What Is Greek Mythology?

by Kathryn Waterfield

illustrated by Gregory Copeland

Penguin Workshop

To Robin, with love—KW

To Rick and Marci—GC

PENGUIN WORKSHOP
An imprint of Penguin Random House LLC
1745 Broadway, New York, NY 10019
penguinrandomhouse.com

Library of Congress Cataloging-in-Publication Data is available.

First published in the United States of America by Penguin Workshop, 2026

Manufactured in the United States of America
CJKW

ISBN 9798217051021 (paperback)
10 9 8 7 6 5 4 3 2 1

ISBN 9798217051038 (library binding)
10 9 8 7 6 5 4 3 2 1

The authorized representative in the EU for product safety and compliance is Penguin Random House Ireland, Morrison Chambers, 32 Nassau Street, Dublin D02 YH68, Ireland, https://eu-contact.penguin.ie.

Contents

What Is Greek Mythology?

Ancient Greece, around 650 BCE. Inside the great hall of the king's palace, in the glow of dozens of torches and oil lamps, one of the king's squires (a young nobleman) presented the famous poet. A seat was offered to him in the center of the hall, where the poet was surrounded by the king and his guests. A table was set beside his chair, with a plate of food and a cup of wine mixed with water.

Another servant handed the poet his lyre, a small stringed instrument like a U-shaped harp.

The king rose, with his cup in hand, and prayed out loud: "I and all those gathered here ask for the blessing of Zeus, so that we may succeed in all we do, and we will honor him and the rest of the gods on Olympus with offerings and sacrifices."

As he finished, everyone tipped their cups so that a few drops of wine from each one spilled to the floor. This was a libation, a way of sharing the wine with the god Zeus as an act of worship and a sign of respect.

After the libation, the feast began. The room was filled with the buzz of conversation and laughter. When everyone had finished, the plates were cleared and the cups refilled. A hush fell on the crowd. All eyes turned to the poet, who sat forward in his chair and plucked briefly at his lyre, checking that it was properly tuned.

The poet lifted his head and called upon the Muse Calliope, the patron goddess of epic poetry, to speak through him: "Sing, Goddess, of the anger of Achilles, son of Peleus, the accursed anger which brought the Achaeans countless agonies and hurled many ghosts of mighty heroes into the Underworld, causing them to become the prey of dogs and carrion birds, and the plan of Zeus was fulfilled . . ."

The poet was reciting from the *Iliad.* It is a tale set in the last year of a decade-long war between the people of Troy, a city in what is today northwestern Turkey, and the Achaeans, from what is now Greece. The *Iliad* and another connected story, the *Odyssey*, are just two of the greatest examples of epic poetry that were told and retold for centuries.

In fact, the scene described above is borrowed from the *Iliad* and *Odyssey* and is not from a recorded historical event. But poetic performances like this happened on thousands of occasions over many generations in ancient Greece. These tales, and many others, taught or reminded the Greeks about how the immortal gods, who held supernatural powers and could not die, were present and involved in human events. They were also fun and exciting, with colorful characters and amazing adventures.

The tales of Greek mythology were embedded in Greek society and were at the center of Greek religion. In time, poets and playwrights wrote down the myths. Some created new stories out of the older ones. Sculptors decorated Greek temples with images of the myths, and artists painted the myths onto vases and walls and etched them onto jewelry. The richness and variety of Greek mythology makes it endlessly adaptable. One story can blend straight away into another. The myths are so attractive that the Romans, the Greeks' Mediterranean neighbors, adapted many of them to their own culture and religion, and from the Romans they came down to us. Over the centuries, Greek mythology has endured, and the stories still captivate us today.

CHAPTER 1
The Storytellers

The ancient Greeks loved telling lively stories and illustrating them in art. The painted pottery they made, especially in Athens, was often completely covered in mythological subjects. They decorated their temples with sculptures that showed myths. Bronze statues of heroes were set up in public spaces. But, for centuries, the myths were not written down. This was because, until around 800 BCE, the ancient Greeks did not have a writing system. Storytellers passed down the myths, generation after generation, by chanting or singing them from memory. One of the first mythical tales that was written down, around 700 BCE, was Homer's epic poem called the *Iliad*.

Homer

The *Iliad* is about the heroes in a war between a Greek army and the city of Troy. At the center of the story is the hero Achilles, the greatest of all the warriors. He quarrels with Agamemnon, the leader of the Greek army. Agamemnon insults Achilles, and so the hero refuses to fight. The story reveals how Achilles's absence from the battlefield affects the lives of both the Greeks and the Trojans. Throughout the *Iliad*, the gods are watching the action unfold. They take sides in the war and interfere in the battles and with one another. Some gods are parents of the heroes. Achilles, for example, is the son of the goddess Thetis and a mortal king, Peleus. Sarpedon, fighting for Troy, is the son of Zeus, the king of the gods.

Throughout the tale, Homer brings to life the horror of war, but he also describes the beauty of love and friendship. The world of the *Iliad* is one where honor is the most important thing. To die an honorable death in battle is better than living to great old age. The *Iliad* was the most important story in ancient Greek civilization. Learning to recite verses from it was one of the foundations of a young Greek's education.

Homer's *Odyssey* was written down not long after the *Iliad*. This poem tells the story of Odysseus, a Greek hero. The *Odyssey* is not about war. The stories it tells are about the dangerous encounters Odysseus and his companions have with a series of fantastic creatures.

Odysseus

The Trojan War is over, and Odysseus and his men want to sail home to their island, Ithaca. But time after time, they are attacked by monsters or witches. Sometimes the gods play with them like toys. The god Poseidon turns against them when Odysseus blinds his giant one-eyed son, the Cyclops Polyphemus, while escaping from the monster. The witch Circe turns some of the men into pigs when they stop at her island.

They encounter the Sirens, half-bird monsters whose sweet feminine singing lures sailors to their deaths. Odysseus is held captive by the nymph

Calypso for years until Zeus orders her to free him. Odysseus finally makes it home with the help of the goddess Athena and is reunited with his wife, Penelope.

Next to Homer in importance to Greek mythology is the poet Hesiod, who lived around the same time as Homer. He wrote an epic poem about the creation of the universe, called *Theogony*. He also wrote another long poem called *Works and Days*. It contains stories about the gods but also offers advice about how to properly manage a farm.

Hesiod

Many storytellers over time built on the work of Homer and Hesiod and imitated their style of writing. A collection of twenty-three poems called the *Homeric Hymns* is an example.

The hymns praise the gods and offer colorful details about them that bring out their personalities. For example, the "Hymn to Demeter" honors the goddess of grain and explains the reason for the seasons. It tells of a famine that Demeter causes when Hades, the god of the Underworld, kidnaps her daughter, Persephone (say: per-SEF-o-nee), to be his wife. Demeter is so upset that she refuses to allow crops to grow. People are starving. Zeus orders Hades to return Persephone to her mother for two-thirds of the year, and Hades agrees. When Persephone goes back to the

Underworld to be with Hades in the winter months, Demeter is so sad that nothing grows. When the girl is allowed to rejoin her mother in the spring, Demeter is happy and the earth becomes fertile again. This shows that the gods' behavior had a profound impact on nature and especially human lives.

Other poets celebrated the best local athletes in praise songs called odes. In these odes, the poet compared a living champion to the heroes of Greek myth. The odes were performed in the victor's community and drew from local myths to tell the stories. In this way, new tales were created from the old ones.

The myths told by Homer and Hesiod were the first to be put in writing. Their versions of Greek gods and heroes were considered the best of a long tradition of oral storytelling. Performances of the epic poems continued long after writing had come to Greece. But the written versions of their epics are the foundation of Greek mythology.

The Greek Alphabet

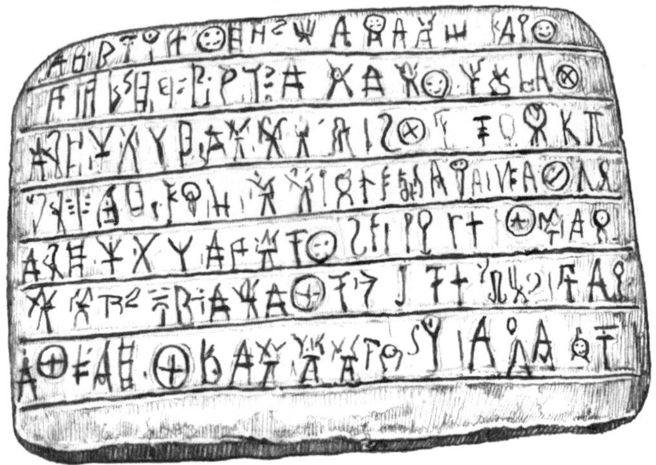

An early form of written Greek

Around 800 BCE, Greek traders brought to Greece a letter-writing system they borrowed from the Phoenicians. The Phoenicians were sailors and merchants from what is now Lebanon. The Phoenician letters, however, did not have any symbols for vowel sounds. So when the Greeks started to use the Phoenician letters to spell

Greek words, they made up vowel symbols. Over time, the alphabet—named for the first two letters of the set of symbols—spread in popularity all over the Greek-speaking world. The Greek alphabet looks like this:

Α	**ALPHA**	Ν	**NU**
Β	**BETA**	Ξ	**KSI**
Γ	**GAMMA**	Ο	**OMICRON**
Δ	**DELTA**	Π	**PI**
Ε	**EPSILON**	Ρ	**RHO**
Ζ	**ZETA**	Σ	**SIGMA**
Η	**ETA**	Τ	**TAU**
Θ	**THETA**	Υ	**UPSILON**
Ι	**IOTA**	Φ	**PHI**
Κ	**KAPPA**	Χ	**CHI**
Λ	**LAMBDA**	Ψ	**PSI**
Μ	**MU**	Ω	**OMEGA**

CHAPTER 2
Creation Myths

From the ninth century BCE (the years 900–801), there was increased contact between Greeks and the kingdoms of Asia Minor (where the continents of Asia and Europe meet, now

Turkey). This increased contact resulted in the importing of not only products such as woven cloth, glass, and ivory but also ideas and stories. The adoption by the Greeks of the Phoenician alphabet and altering it to suit their own language is one important example. The creation stories Hesiod told are another, drawn from much older stories from the east. He shaped them into something suited to the Greeks' beliefs.

In *Theogony*, the creation myth began with Chaos, a swirling black nothingness, which was one of the first beings to exist. Suddenly the goddess Gaia (say: GY-a), the personification of Earth, appeared. Gaia made the god Pontus, the endless expanse of the sea, and she caused the mountains to rise up. Pontus and Gaia together had five children, who were the first gods of the sea. These sea gods were the parents of many sea monsters and nymphs (less important goddesses).

Out of the confusion of Chaos, a natural order began to form. The passing of time became marked by the periods of day and night.

Gaia joined with the god Uranus, who was the sky. Among their children were the Titans. These early gods were cruel and jealous. Cronus took power from his father, Uranus. He ruled for a time and had six children by his sister Rhea. But Cronus was a heartless father, and his children rebelled against him. Led by Zeus, and with some of the other Titans as allies, they defeated Cronus and took over the universe. The enemy Titans were sent to Tartarus, the deepest part of the Underworld, where they could never escape. But one of them—Atlas—was punished by having to support the sky on his shoulders for all time.

Hesiod's *Works and Days* contains a myth about the five ages of humankind. The first was the age of the Golden Generation. These humans had an easy life with no hard work. They interacted freely with the gods. But they had no children, so they became extinct. The Silver Generation that Zeus made next were not very smart. They were also violent. They did not worship the gods, so Zeus destroyed them. The Bronze Generation grew no crops and did nothing but wage war. Zeus lost his patience with them and sent a great flood to sweep them all away.

Hesiod's fourth age was the time of the heroes. While they made war against each other like the Bronze Generation, some accomplished great deeds and valued honor. The final age of humankind in Hesiod's story was the one in which he was living—the Age of Iron. It was a time when people struggled to produce enough food to survive (iron was the metal used to create tools of hard labor, like plows, axes, and saws). Unlike the Heroic Age, there was no longer a strong code of honor, although Hesiod believed in it himself. He thought people should worship the gods to gain their support, because life was difficult and humans needed all the help they could get.

One of the greatest allies of humankind in Greek mythology was Prometheus. He and his brother Epimetheus were two of the Titans who fought with Zeus against their brother Cronus.

Prometheus

Prometheus had a soft spot for humankind. He felt sorry for them because they had no protection against the elements and dangerous animals. He convinced Zeus to give them fire.

With it they could make weapons and pottery, warm themselves from the cold, light the dark, and cook their food. Fire is the foundation of civilization.

Zeus wanted humans to use fire to make burnt offerings for the gods. He asked Prometheus to butcher an ox and divide the portions. Zeus would choose which one was to be offered to the gods and which would be eaten by humans. Prometheus tricked Zeus by wrapping the inedible bones in fat. The meat he wrapped in the ox's hide. Zeus thought the fat-wrapped bones looked better, so he chose them for the gods' offering.

Prometheus was pleased that humans would get the nourishing meat and protective hide. When Zeus discovered Prometheus's trick, he took away fire from the world and hid it on Mount Olympus. But Prometheus stole a bit of it and gave it back to humans. As punishment, Zeus chained him to a mountain, where every day an eagle came and ate his liver, which grew back again every night.

With creation complete, the gods gathered at their headquarters on Mount Olympus. They held an assembly, where it was decided what roles they would play in life on earth. A great palace was built for their home. The gods who chose to live at the palace are known as the Olympians.

CHAPTER 3
The Olympians

The Olympian gods described by Homer and Hesiod were a clan made up of the brothers and sisters of Zeus and his children. Greek mythology is full of stories about how they argued, lied to each other, and played pranks. But they worked together, too, as when they defeated a race of giants sent by Gaia to challenge their rule.

Each member had a job overseeing an aspect of life on earth. Most of them have attributes—symbols—that illustrate that role.

Zeus was the most powerful of them all and king of the gods. As ruler of the heavens, his weapon, the lightning bolt, is his symbol. Poseidon was appointed master of the land and sea. His attribute is the trident, a three-pronged fishing spear.

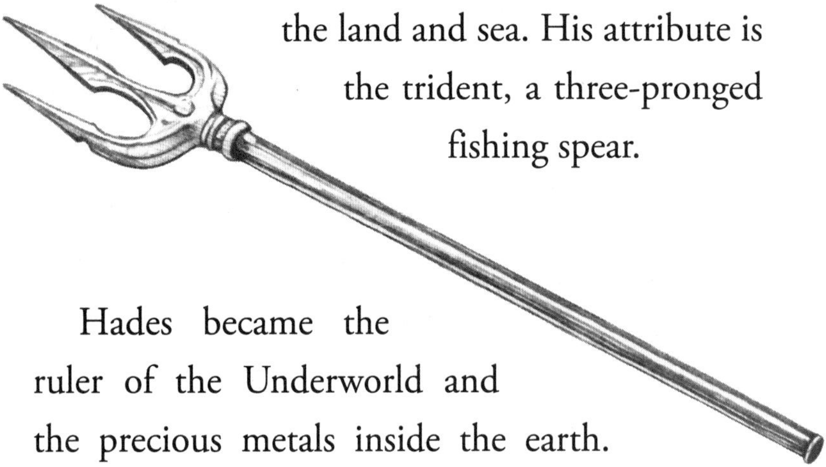

Hades became the ruler of the Underworld and the precious metals inside the earth. He carries a scepter, a royal staff. Zeus's sister Hestia was given oversight of the hearths and homes of humankind as well as the sacred fire on Olympus. She is not depicted with any symbols.

Hestia

One of the wives of Zeus was Metis, whose name means "wisdom" in Greek. She was one of the Titans who helped Zeus in the war against Cronus. But Zeus had heard that any child he had with Metis would be greater than him. So when Metis told him she was pregnant, he swallowed her. When it was time for the baby to be born, it popped out of Zeus's head! It was Athena, fully grown and already wearing her armor. Athena was the goddess of wisdom and warcraft. She was also the goddess of crafts like weaving and pottery. She is often shown with an owl and wearing a helmet and carrying a spear. Zeus married his sister, Hera, and she became queen of the gods. She was the goddess of marriage. Her symbol is the peacock.

Athena, Goddess of Wisdom and War

Together they had four children: daughters Hebe (say: HE-bee) and Eileithyia (say: ee-LEE-thee-a), and sons Ares (say: AIR-ees) and Hephaestus (say: he-FEYS-tus). The daughters were goddesses of homemaking and childbirth. They have no symbols to mark them out. Ares, the god of war, is always shown in full armor. Hephaestus was the god of metalworking. He had a lame foot, which was injured when Zeus, angry over Hephaestus's meddling in a quarrel with Hera, tossed him down from Mount Olympus. His symbols are a hammer or an ax and the felt cap that blacksmiths wore.

Symbol of Hephaestus, God of Metalworking

Zeus's sister Demeter was the goddess of grain. She carries a sheaf of grain stalks. Their daughter, Persephone, was the embodiment of spring. Persephone's symbol is the pomegranate.

Apollo and Artemis

Clever Hermes was the son of Zeus and a nymph, Maia (say: MY-ah). He was the gods' messenger, shown with his winged sandals and snake-entwined staff. The Titan Leto was the mother of Zeus's twins Artemis and Apollo. Artemis was the goddess of wild animals, young girls, and archery. She is always shown with her bow and arrows. Apollo was the god of prophecy, healing, and the arts. Like his sister, he carries a bow, and often a lyre.

Zeus's son Dionysus was born from a mortal woman, Semele (say: SEM-eh-lee), who was later made immortal. Dionysus was the god of wine, feasting, and theater. He often ran wild in the forests of the earth. His female companions, the maenads (say: MY-nads) and his half-goat male followers, the satyrs, accompanied him. His attributes are a staff wound with ivy and a wreath of grape leaves.

Then, finally, there was Aphrodite, the daughter of Zeus and the Titan Dione. She was the goddess of beauty and desire. In art, Eros, the god of love, is often shown by her side. Two of her attributes are the dove and the rose.

There were, of course, many other immortals, like the Muses, who, with Apollo, oversaw the arts and culture.

The Fates decided the length of a human life. Helios drove the chariot of the sun from east to west every day. But the Olympians were the gods who were most worshipped by the Greeks and were central to Greek religion.

CHAPTER 4
Greek Mythology and Religion

The ancient Greeks believed that the gods were real and worshipped them with prayers and rituals. Each god was prayed to according to their role as an overseer of some aspect of human life. Zeus would be called upon for fair weather. Farmers prayed to Demeter for a good harvest.

Prayers for a healthy baby were made to Eileithyia. Potters and weavers made offerings to Athena to bless their craftsmanship. If a disease struck, prayers for a cure would be made to Apollo and Artemis. Sailors asked Poseidon to protect them from being shipwrecked. A young bride and groom prayed to Hera to bless their marriage.

Prayers and worship usually came with an offering to the gods. Hestia might be offered a libation or a handful of herbs thrown into the flames of her hearth. Aphrodite's altar might receive a wreath of flowers.

In Poseidon's temples, sailors prayed to the god and left behind an offering such as a small ship figurine made of clay or metal.

On important religious occasions, an animal was sacrificed. The animal—an ox, perhaps—was brought forward to the altar outside the temple, the place where the gods were worshipped. After the ox was slaughtered, it was skinned and butchered. The bones were wrapped in fat and placed on the altar fire, the way Hesiod described it in the story of Prometheus's trick on Zeus. As the burning fat sent smoke into the air, prayers were made to the god. It was believed that the smell of the burnt offering and the smoke got the gods' attention. People hoped that the gods would be pleased and answer their prayers. Special portions of the meat were given to the priests who led the ceremony. The rest was cooked and shared by the worshippers, much like a public barbecue.

Hulton Archive/Getty Images

Statue of the Greek playwright Euripides

Culture Club/Hulton Fine Art Collection/Getty Images

A temple dedicated to Athena on the Acropolis in Athens, Greece

Photo Researchers/Archive Photos/Getty Images

Hades, the god of the Underworld, and his three-headed dog, Cerberus

Statue of Athena, the goddess of wisdom and war

Sculpture of the Greek epic poet Homer

PHAS/Universal Images Group/Getty Images

Statue of Demeter, the goddess of grain

The statue of Zeus at Olympia,
print by Philips Galle and Maarten van Heemskerck, 1572

Medusa's death, painting by Caravaggio, 1597

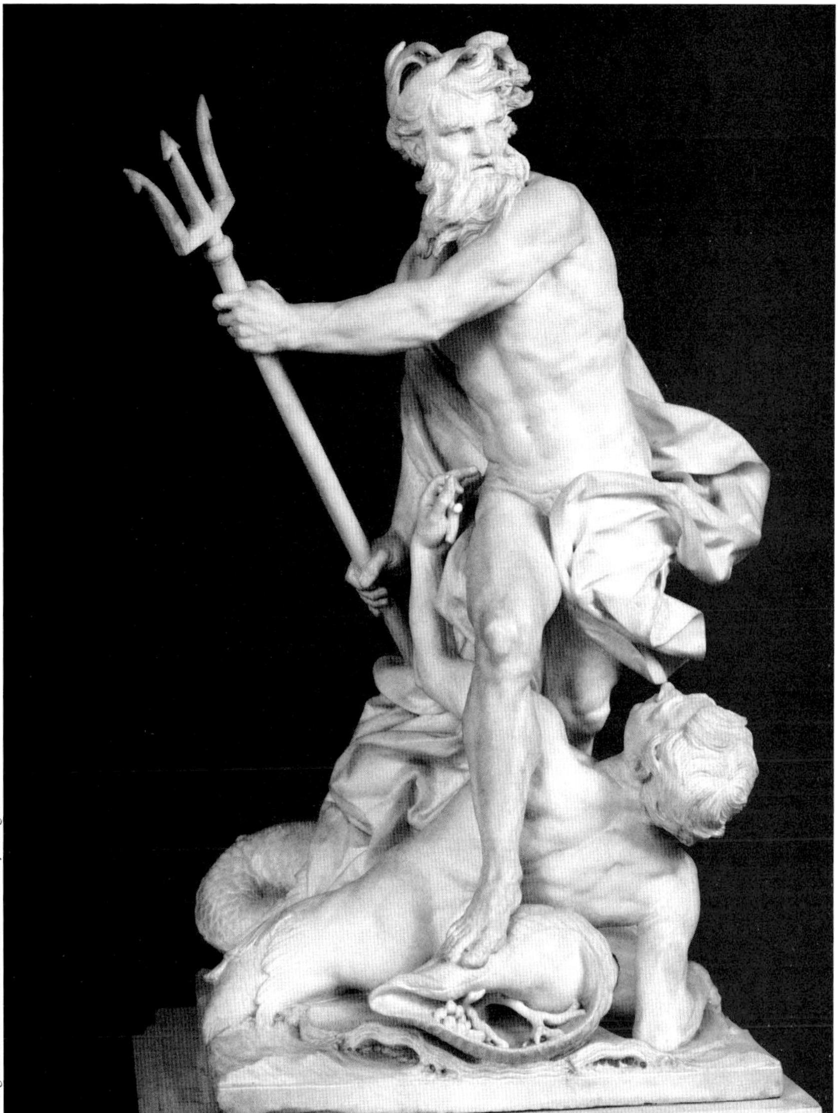

Neptune Calming the Waves, statue by Lambert-Sigisbert Adam, 1737

Perseus armed by nymphs and wearing winged sandals from Hermes, illustration by Walter Crane, 1852

The king of Iolcus sending Jason to find the Golden Fleece

Paul Popper/Popperfoto/Getty Images

Ruins of the Theater of Dionysus

The Olympic torch being lit in Olympia before it's carried to Mexico City for the 1968 Olympic Games

Anadolu/Getty Images

The tomb of Heracles on display in Turkey

George Pachantouris/Moment/Getty Images

The Acropolis in Athens, Greece

Milos Bicanski/Getty Images News/Getty Images

Tourists gathering at the Parthenon

Greece

There were places across Greece that became centers of worship for certain gods. Greeks would gather from near and far to hold festivals with contests in the god's honor. One of the most important of these places was Olympia, in southwestern Greece. Olympia was special to Zeus and was the home of the Olympic Games, founded in 776 BCE. The Games were held every four years. At first, the only event was a footrace. Over time, the Olympics expanded to twenty-three events, including boxing, wrestling, chariot races, and a footrace in full armor—all for the greater glory of Zeus.

The opening ceremony of the Olympic Games took place before the Temple of Zeus, which held a forty-foot-tall gold-and-ivory statue

of the god seated on his throne. On the second day of the Olympics, a hundred oxen were sacrificed at the altar outside Zeus's temple. The prize for winning an event was a wreath of olive leaves and great fame throughout Greece. Many of the winners' names were inscribed in stone at the site and can still be seen today.

The Olympic Games became the most important event in the ancient Greek world and lasted until the fifth century CE (the years 400–499).

At Delphi in central Greece, the Pythian Games were held in honor of Apollo. In Greek mythology, Apollo founded Delphi when he killed a monstrous serpent there, the Python. Inside Apollo's temple sat a priestess called the Pythia. She was Apollo's oracle. An oracle was a person who acted as a sort of messenger between the gods and the people. The Pythia provided answers from Apollo in response to questions people asked about their problems. The oracle at Delphi was so famous that even non-Greek people came to consult Apollo through the Pythia. The Pythian Games began as music contests, but later most of the Olympic events were added. The winners were awarded a wreath from the bay laurel, the tree sacred to Apollo.

Athens held a yearly festival called the Panathenaea in honor of its patron goddess, Athena. In Greek mythology, Athena won a contest with Poseidon to be the city's patron.

With his trident, Poseidon struck the bedrock of the Acropolis, the highest point in the city, and a spring bubbled up. Athena caused an olive tree to grow there. Athena won the contest because the people preferred the olive tree to the spring, which, coming from the god of the sea, tasted salty!

Founded in 566 BCE, every four years the Panathenaea was expanded into a larger festival that may have lasted for as long as twelve days. The events included footraces and a chariot race. There were singing and poetry contests that included the reciting of sections from the *Iliad* and the *Odyssey*. The winners were awarded jars of olive oil from Athena's sacred grove. At the end of the festival, a great procession carried an ancient wooden statue of the goddess up to Athena's temple, the Parthenon, high on the Acropolis. Young women dressed the statue in a newly woven garment called a peplos. Then more than one hundred sheep and oxen were sacrificed to the goddess.

There were other festivals in addition to these examples. Nearly every Greek city had a celebration to honor its patron god or goddess, just as Athena was the protector of Athens. Cities also honored the heroes, who were the children of immortals and humans. The hero Heracles, for example, was honored in many Greek cities, but especially at Thebes, where he was said to have been born. A tomb-like building was constructed for the hero.

Tomb of Heracles

Worshippers came to the hero's "tomb" to make prayers and offerings. The Greeks believed that if they pleased the hero by their worship, the hero would influence the gods in their favor. The heroes' condition of being demigods—half god and half human—made them well suited for such a role.

The Parthenon

The Parthenon was built between 447 and 432 BCE. It is called the Parthenon after Athena Parthenos, which is Greek for "the Maiden."

In ancient times, the temple held a thirty-eight-foot-tall statue of the goddess. It was made of ivory and gold, like the one of Zeus at Olympia. The outside of the temple had sculptures carved all the way around the upper part of the building, a few of which are still in place on the ruined temple. They showed mythological scenes such as the Trojan War and the gods battling the giants. In the pediments, the triangular spaces on top of the columns at each end, more sculptures were carved. One group showed the myth of Athena's birth from the head of Zeus. The other depicted the contest for Athens between Poseidon and Athena. Every sculpture would have been brightly painted, making for a very colorful and vivid display.

CHAPTER 5
Heroes and Their Deeds

Some of the most colorful and exciting stories in Greek mythology are the adventures of the heroes. They are the stories most often depicted on ancient Greek pottery. An important written source for the hero myths is the *Bibliotheca* (Greek for "library") of Apollodorus. It was probably written in the late first century CE (the years 1–100). He collected the Greek myths from many earlier sources and put them together like an encyclopedia.

A modern translation of the *Bibliotheca* of Apollodorus

Some of the many famous Greek hero myths are Perseus and the Gorgon Medusa, Jason and the Argonauts, Theseus and the Minotaur, and Bellerophon and the winged horse Pegasus. There is also Atalanta, one of the few female heroes. She was a huntress who brought down a giant boar (wild pig) that was causing destruction in Calydon, in central Greece. And then there is Heracles, the most famous hero in Greek mythology.

Perseus was the son of Zeus and the princess Danaë (say: DAN-eye) of Argos in southern Greece. Danaë's father heard a prophecy that his grandson would kill him. So he locked Perseus and his mother in a wooden chest and cast them into the sea. They washed up on the island of Seriphus. But the evil king of the island wanted Danaë for himself. To get rid of Perseus, he ordered him to find the Gorgon Medusa and bring back her head. Athena and Hermes gave Perseus help with his quest. Hermes loaned Perseus his winged sandals so he could fly and a cap of invisibility. Athena loaned him her shield and a magic satchel in which to carry the monster's head.

There were three Gorgons, whose gazes turned people into stone. They had snakes for hair, long fangs, and sharp claws. Wings of gold sprouted from their backs. But only Medusa was mortal. Wearing his magic cap, Perseus sneaked into the Gorgons' cave and found them asleep. He used the shield to see Medusa's reflection instead of looking at her directly. He cut off the monster's head and placed it in the satchel. When the other two Gorgons saw what he had done, they chased after him, but he escaped using Hermes's winged sandals. He flew back to Seriphus, where he showed Medusa's head to the king. The king instantly turned to stone. Perseus gave the Gorgon's head to Athena, and she placed it over the breastplate of her armor.

Jason was the rightful heir to the kingdom of

Iolcus (say: EYE-ol-kus), in eastern Greece. He was the great-grandson of Hermes and a favorite of Hera. Jason's uncle stole the throne from his father and sent him and young Jason away. At Iolcus, the king heard a prophecy that a stranger wearing one sandal would come and take his throne. Jason returned to Iolcus when he was grown, and along the way lost one of his sandals.

The king saw the one-sandaled stranger and remembered the prophecy. So the king sent Jason on a quest for the Golden Fleece (a sheepskin that symbolized a king's right to rule). If Jason completed this difficult task, the king promised to hand over the throne of Iolcus. This was a lie. The king believed that Jason would fail his quest.

The Golden Fleece was guarded by a dragon in the royal forest of the king of Colchis (say: kol-KEES), far to the east of Greece. To help, Athena had a magical talking ship built for Jason, the *Argo*, and he set sail with his team of heroes, the Argonauts. After many adventures and encounters with monsters, they arrived. The king plotted to kill Jason, but his daughter, the witch Medea, helped the hero to destroy the dragon and take the fleece. The Argonauts and Medea returned to Iolcus, where Medea used her magic to trick the king's daughters into boiling him in a giant pot.

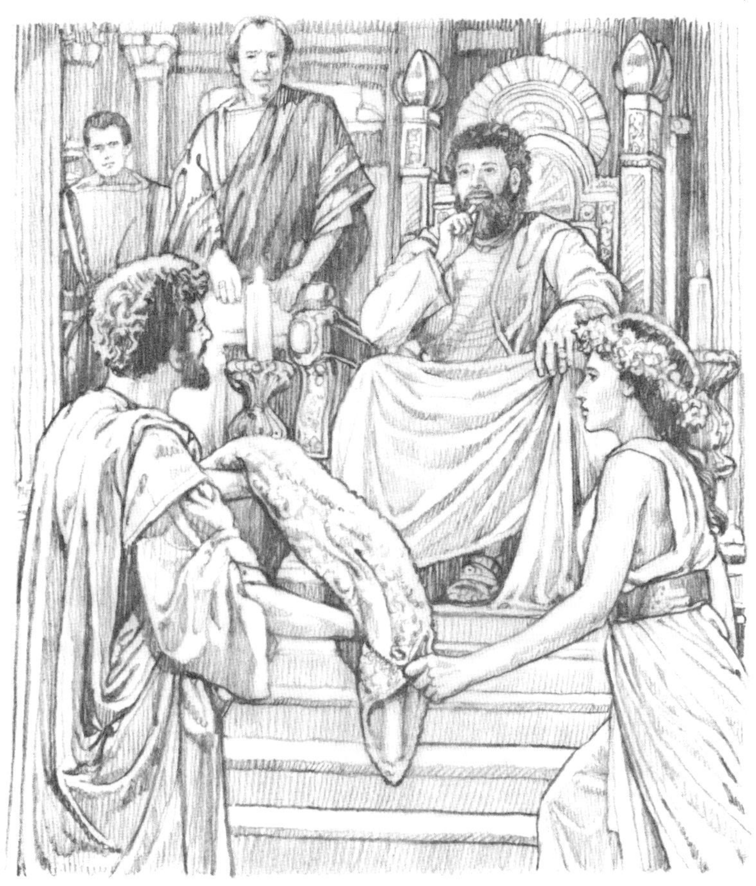

Bellerophon, a prince of Corinth in southern Greece, was a son of Poseidon. After accidentally killing his brother, he was sent away. He arrived in Lycia, a kingdom in what is now southern Turkey. The Lycian king commanded him to destroy the

Chimera (say: KY-me-ra). The Chimera was a fire-breathing monster with a lion's head, a goat's body, and a serpent's tail. It would not be easy to kill.

Poseidon helped his son by giving him Pegasus, the winged white horse. Pegasus was untamed, so Athena gave Bellerophon a magic bridle with which to control the horse. Together the hero and the flying horse defeated the Chimera. In thanks, the Lycian king gave Bellerophon half of his kingdom.

Theseus, a prince of Athens, was also a son of Poseidon. Theseus sailed to the island of Crete to save Athenian children who were taken by Minos, the Cretan king. Every year, Minos demanded seven boys and seven girls in order to feed them to the Minotaur. The Minotaur was a monster that had a man's body and the head of a bull. The Minotaur was imprisoned in a maze of corridors beneath the palace called the Labyrinth. Theseus swore he would find his way through the Labyrinth and kill the Minotaur.

King Minos's daughter Ariadne fell in love with Theseus. To help him destroy the monster, she gave him a glowing spool of thread. As Theseus moved through the Labyrinth, he unspooled the thread so that he could find his way back out. He succeeded in killing the Minotaur and sailed away from Crete with the children and Ariadne.

Heracles

Heracles is better known today by his Roman name, Hercules. He was the son of Zeus and Alcmene (say: alk-ME-nee), a princess of Mycenae (say: my-SEE-nee) in southern Greece. The hero grew up and developed superhuman strength. But jealous Hera resented Heracles, so she caused him to accidentally kill his own wife and children. As punishment, Heracles was sent to serve his cousin Eurystheus (say: you-RIS-thee-us), the king of Tiryns. He was required to do anything his cousin asked for twelve years. The tasks assigned to him are known as "Heracles's Twelve Labors."

His early tasks were to clear the Peloponnese, the large peninsula of southern Greece, from dangerous creatures. The first task, or labor, he was given was to kill a vicious lion prowling the area. No weapons would work against the beast, so Heracles wrestled it with his bare hands. He skinned the strangled lion and wore its pelt as a cloak. The head and jaws were his helmet. The lionskin and a giant wooden club were his attributes, and in art, he is always shown with them.

Heracles accomplished another task when he caught a giant wild boar that was rampaging through the countryside. He trapped the boar and brought it back to Tiryns. Eurystheus was so afraid when he saw it that he hid in a giant storage jar.

The later labors of Heracles had him traveling far and wide. He was ordered to fight the queen of the warrior women, the Amazons. Heracles kidnapped the queen's sister and demanded a magic belt as ransom. The queen paid the ransom, but later he killed her during a battle.

Heracles's final labor was to enter the Underworld and steal Cerberus, the three-headed hound of Hades. Cerberus stood guard over the shores of the River Styx, the boundary of the Underworld, to keep any souls from escaping.

Heracles pinned Cerberus down and dragged it away with a triple-stranded leash. Persephone and Hades were angry that Heracles stole their watchdog. But Hermes explained to them that it would be returned. When Heracles brought the monster hound to Tiryns, Eurystheus was so scared he jumped back into his giant jar! True to his word, Heracles returned Cerberus to the Underworld. He had completed his twelve years of service and atoned for the killing of his wife and children.

The Amazons

The Amazons were female warriors and hunters, said to be from Pontus on the Black Sea. They were famous for their skill in combat, especially on horseback. Men were excluded from their society. They often chose kings or heroes to father their children, such as when Antiope (say: an-TY-o-pea) chose Theseus. They raised only their daughters and returned any sons to their fathers.

It is possible that Amazons in Greek mythology were inspired by the real horse-riding culture of the Eurasian Steppe (grasslands of eastern Europe and north Asia). In 2019, a grave with several generations of warrior women, buried with their weapons and wearing gold headdresses, was discovered in southwestern Russia.

The Greek hero myths are exciting stories, full of adventure. But to the ancient Greeks, the heroes symbolized humankind's growth from primitive ways to civilized ones. Heroes like Heracles, Perseus, and others conquered the uncivilized parts of the world and its monsters. But when heroes committed a crime, they paid a price, even though they were the children of gods. And in spite of the heroes' great deeds, if they angered the gods, the result could be a tragedy.

CHAPTER 6
Greek Drama

Greek drama grew out of the tradition of reciting epic poetry. Athens was famous for its dramatic contests. Every spring, Athens held the City Dionysia in honor of the god Dionysus. In 534 BCE, it was expanded into a weeklong festival that began with a procession carrying the god's statue to the Theater of Dionysus below the Acropolis. Three days of the festival were reserved for the performance of sets of three tragedies (trilogies) followed by a fourth, lighthearted performance called a satyr play. A tragedy is a story about the downfall of a character or characters who have offended the gods. The cast of the earliest plays were the chorus, who narrated the story, and a single actor playing a role or roles.

The most famous tragic playwrights were Aeschylus (say: EES-ke-lus), Sophocles (say: SOF-o-klees), and Euripides (say: you-RI-peh-dees). They all lived during the fifth century BCE, which is considered the golden age of Greek drama.

Aeschylus (525–456 BCE) was the inventor of the trilogy. One of his trilogies, the *Oresteia*, is the only complete set to have come down to modern times. It won the drama prize at the City Dionysia in 458. The theme of the *Oresteia* is that taking the law into one's own hands is bad for society.

Aeschylus

In *Agamemnon*, the first play of the trilogy, the war is over and the king of Mycenae returns home after defeating the Trojans. The queen Clytemnestra (say: kly-tem-NES-tra) kills Agamemnon because he sacrificed their daughter Iphigenia (say: iph-i-je-NYA), to the goddess Artemis before he set off for Troy.

The Ancient Greek Theater

Ancient Greek theaters were ideally located on a sloping hill that provided natural seating. Otherwise, wooden bleachers were installed. This seating area was called the theatron, Greek for "place for seeing." The Theater of Dionysus in Athens could seat ten thousand people. At the base of the theatron was the orchestra, or "dancing place," a flat circular space where the plays were staged. After 465 BCE, a framed canvas, called the skene (say: skee-NEE), was added as a backdrop. Behind this panel, actors could change costumes or wait for their entrance. Later, the skene was made permanent and built to resemble the front of a building, and a low stage was added. All the actors and chorus members wore masks and costumes that identified their characters. The masks had large eye and mouth openings so that the actors could see and be heard. Only men performed in ancient Greek drama, even playing the female roles.

Greek theaters spread all over the Mediterranean world. They were so popular that they became one of the key buildings of a Greek city. A few ancient theaters have been restored and host performances even today.

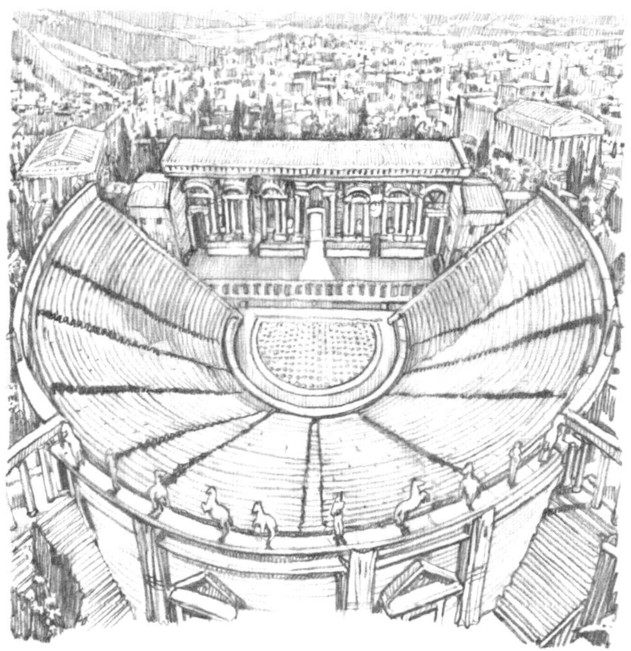

The Theater of Dionysus

In *Libation Bearers*, Orestes, the son of Agamemnon and the queen, returns to Mycenae after some years have passed. Apollo has commanded him to avenge his father's death.

He meets his sister Electra, praying and making libations at their father's tomb. Together the siblings take revenge on their mother.

The third play, *Eumenides*, tells the story

of what Orestes suffers for killing his mother. The Furies are harassing Orestes. They are the goddesses who pursue and punish those who kill their relatives. Orestes escapes them with the help of Apollo and Hermes. He goes to Athens, where he begs Athena for help. The goddess arranges a trial with twelve judges, but they are evenly split in their verdict. Athena breaks the tie with her vote, and Orestes is pardoned. The Furies are of course furious. But Athena persuades them that law and order are better solutions to conflict. This tames the Furies, and they become the Eumenides, which in Greek means "the kindly ones."

Sophocles

The career of Sophocles (496–405 BCE) overlapped those of Aeschylus and Euripides. He wrote more than 120 plays, but only seven have survived to the present day. Over fifty years, Sophocles competed in thirty drama contests and won twenty-four, in at least one case by beating Aeschylus. Sophocles added a third actor onstage for his plays. Previously, Aeschylus had added a second actor and reduced the chorus from fifty to twelve players. Having up to three actors onstage increased the dramatic possibilities.

Euripides

Euripides (480–406 BCE) is the playwright with the most surviving tragedies: eighteen. He wrote several plays on the topic of Agamemnon's family. One of them is *Iphigenia in Aulis.* The play is set before the Trojan War. Agamemnon learns that the fleet cannot sail for Troy. Artemis is angry with him for killing a sacred stag while out hunting. She will not allow good sailing winds until he sacrifices his daughter Iphigenia. The king sends a message to Clytemnestra to bring the girl to Aulis, on the east coast of Greece, where the army has gathered. He lies to the queen, saying that Iphigenia is to marry the hero Achilles, so she will not object. Once the truth is out, Iphigenia begs her father not to sacrifice her. But in the end, she changes her mind and heroically dies on the altar.

The surviving plays of Aeschylus, Sophocles, and Euripides are still produced today. This shows how the characters they wrote about—people who make terrible mistakes and pay the price for it—matter over time and cultures. People will always struggle with telling right from wrong. The stories from Greek mythology are a useful tool to express this struggle and comment on human choices.

CHAPTER 7
Transformations

Transformations (dramatic changes or alterations) occur frequently in Greek mythology. These changes generally happen when one of the gods is offended or rejected by a human, and that human is turned into something else—a plant, an animal, even a constellation of stars. The best ancient collection of transformation myths was written by the Roman poet Ovid, who was born in 43 BCE.

Ovid

Ovid wrote down a great many of the Greek myths in a poem called *Metamorphoses*, the Greek word for "transformations."

The poem contains more than 250 myths, beginning with the creation myth, which describes the change from Chaos to Order first told by Hesiod. Ovid cleverly connected each of the myths together to make one overall story with a beginning, middle, and end.

For example, after the creation story and the myth of the Ages of Humankind, Ovid added details to the story of the great flood that Zeus sent to destroy the Bronze Generation. Zeus had allowed only two people to survive the flood: Deucalion, the son of Prometheus, and Pyrrha, the daughter of Epimetheus. The task of repopulating the earth fell to them. But they were old and could not have children. They prayed to their parents to help them accomplish Zeus's assignment. In reply, they were told to throw stones behind them as they walked about. The stones softened and reshaped into human form, making a new race of men. These were the men and women of the Heroic Age.

Some transformation myths explain how something came to be. The story of the constellations called Ursa Major and Ursa Minor is about how jealous Hera turned the nymph Callisto into a bear for having a son of Zeus, named Arcas. When he was grown, Arcas came upon Callisto while hunting in the woods. Not knowing it was his mother, the young man took aim at the bear. But before Arcas could shoot, Zeus took them both and put them in the night sky as the Great Bear and the Lesser Bear constellations.

Another myth tells of when the talented weaver Arachne (say: a-RAK-nee) challenged Athena to a contest of skill. This angered the goddess, but she accepted the challenge. Both the girl and the goddess wove beautiful tapestries, and Athena could find no flaw in Arachne's work. But for committing the sin of pride, Athena turned Arachne into the first spider, forever spinning her web.

A transformation could also be self-inflicted, as it is in the myth of Narcissus. He was a very handsome young hunter. But he refused to marry. One day in the woods, he sat down by a pool of clear water to rest. He saw his reflection in the pool—and instantly fell in love! He tried again and again to touch the face in the pool, but it was always out of reach. He could not eat or drink in his grief. In the end, he died of a broken heart. In his place by the pool sprouted the flower that bears his name. And today, when we describe someone who loves only themself, we call them a narcissist.

Sometimes the transformation is a gift, not a punishment. Pygmalion was a talented artist. Every day he worked in his studio on a statue of the finest white marble. Slowly he shaped the form of a woman from the stone. It was so lifelike that Pygmalion dressed it and gave it a name, Galatea. Pygmalion prayed in Aphrodite's temple for a solution to his lovesick condition.

The goddess answered his prayer. When he returned to his studio, he was amazed to see Galatea had come to life.

The story of Midas is a myth in which the human, rather than the gods, does the transforming. Midas was the king of Phrygia, in what is today central Turkey. One day the king was walking in his garden and came upon a satyr (a woodland god) asleep on the ground. He recognized the satyr as Silenus (say: sy-LEE-nus), the old teacher of Dionysus. He returned Silenus to the god, and in gratitude Dionysus offered to grant him a favor.

Midas asked that he be given the power to turn whatever he touched into gold. The god granted his wish, but it was more of a curse than a blessing. Sticks and stones became gold at his touch. The door of his palace, the bed he slept on, everything transformed. At dinner, he tried to eat his meal, but golden meat and wine were inedible.

In despair, he cried out to Dionysus to release him from his "gift," and the god consented. And today, if someone has the ability to make a lot of money, we say that person has "the Midas touch."

CHAPTER 8
Greek Mythology after the Greeks

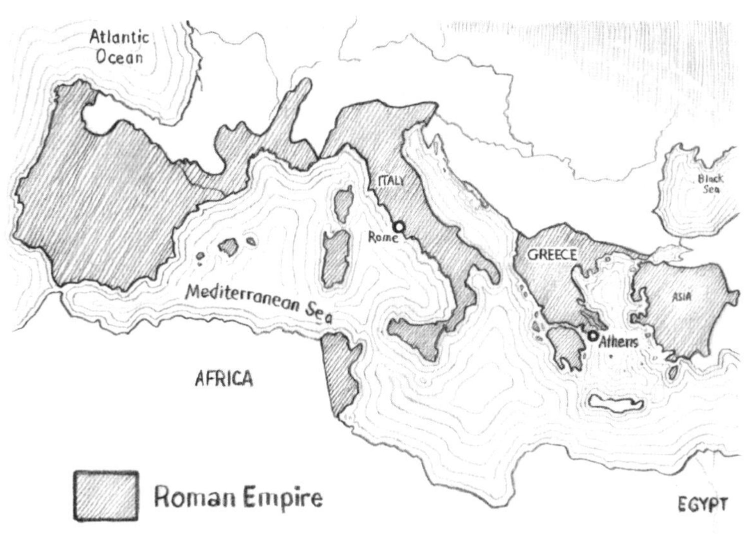

The Roman Empire in 100 BCE

Greek mythology itself was transformed over the centuries, beginning with the Roman adoption of Greek literature. By 100 BCE, the warlike Romans had conquered much of the Mediterranean world. Even before they conquered

Greece, the Romans had admired Greek culture for a long time. They adapted Greek mythology to their own religion. Greek Zeus was Roman Jupiter, Hera was called Juno, Aphrodite was Venus, and so on. Eventually Roman writers like Ovid made their own myths based on the Greek ones.

Virgil

Toward the end of the first century BCE (the years 100–1), the Roman poet Virgil wrote the *Aeneid* to explain the mythical origins of the Roman people and their destiny as rulers of the known world. It is a sequel to the *Iliad*, like the *Odyssey*. Unlike the Greek *Iliad*, the Roman *Aeneid* describes the end of the Trojan War, including the story of the Trojan horse. In the *Aeneid*, the hero, Aeneas, is a prince of the city of Troy and the son of Aphrodite. He survives the war and sails away.

Along the way, he has adventures that resemble those of Odysseus. He finally settles in Italy, where he becomes the ancestor of the Roman people.

The western part of the Roman Empire declined from the fifth century CE (the years 401–500) onward due to invasions from outsiders. The cities were crumbling and in disrepair, and people left them for the countryside. Disease caused the population of Europe to shrink. The few remaining literate people (those who could read) were Christian priests and monks. They maintained libraries and copied Greek and Latin literature, including the myths. This preserved them for future generations, when a reawakening of learning would come.

That reawakening is called the Renaissance ("rebirth" in French). In Europe, this was the beginning of a renewed interest in the ancient Greek myths and literature, as well as ancient Greek and Roman art. It inspired artists like

Sandro Botticelli (1445–1510) to make art based on Greek mythological characters. In 1485, for example, he painted his beautiful and mysterious *Birth of Venus*.

The Trojan Horse

At Troy, the Greeks became impatient to end the war, and scheming Odysseus came up with a plan to trick the Trojans. The Greeks built a tall, hollow-bodied wooden horse. A group of warriors climbed inside. The Greeks left the giant horse at the gates of Troy, claiming it was an offering to Athena. Then they sailed away. The Trojans decided to bring the horse inside the city as a trophy for what they thought was their victory. At nightfall, the hidden Greek soldiers climbed out of the horse and ambushed the Trojans. The rest of the Greek army sailed back to Troy and destroyed the city.

In the eighteenth and nineteenth centuries, Greek and Roman literature was at the heart of university studies in Europe and America. This in turn brought about an interest by scholars in locating the places where events occurred in Greek mythology. They wanted to prove that myths like the *Iliad* were not complete fiction. A wealthy German, Heinrich Schliemann, uncovered the ancient cities of Troy and Mycenae in the 1870s. For his work he is called the Father of Mediterranean Archaeology.

Heinrich Schliemann

There was also a surge of interest in reviving Greek drama. The first modern professional performance of a Greek tragedy was held in Athens in 1867. It was a play by Sophocles called *Antigone* and, unlike the ancient custom, was performed with women in the female roles.

In modern times, the Greek myths are as popular as ever. In literature, the scholar Edith Hamilton published *Mythology: Timeless Tales of Gods and Heroes* in 1942. Robert Graves published his collection, *The Greek Myths*, in 1955.

One of the most successful recent adaptations of the Greek myths for younger readers is the Percy Jackson and the Olympians books written by Rick Riordan. The books are set in a world where the Greek gods exist in the twenty-first century. The main character, Percy, is the son of Poseidon. With his best friends Grover, a satyr, and Annabeth, a daughter of Athena, he embarks on adventures that include retrieving Zeus's lightning bolt and the Golden Fleece. Some of the many mythological characters who appear in the books include the Cyclops Polyphemus, the Oracle of Delphi, and the Sirens. Percy Jackson and the Olympians has been adapted into movies, a musical play, and a television series.

Comic book superheroes like Wonder Woman are inspired by Greek gods or heroes. Wonder Woman's "real" name is Diana, the Roman name of Artemis. Wonder Woman first appeared in the eighth issue of *All Star Comics* in 1941. Since then, the character has appeared in television series, movies, and video games.

Video games inspired by the Greek myths include *The Battle of Olympus* (1988), *Age of Mythology: The Titans* (2003), and *A Total War Saga: Troy* (2020). Dozens of movies have been made that feature Greek myths. Among them are *Jason and the Argonauts* (1963), *Troy* (2004), *Clash of the Titans* (1981, 2010), and *Immortals* (2011). Unsurprisingly, the most popular mythological subject in films is Heracles/Hercules. More than fifty films or television series featuring him have been produced since the 1950s.

Hercules film by Disney released in 1997

The ancient Greeks were thrilled by the myths the storytellers recited. Because the myths were written down, it became possible to create collections of stories that were connected by their shared characters—the heroes and the gods, the kings and queens, and the fantastic creatures. These stories continue to excite our imaginations. Over centuries, storytellers altered the myths to suit their times. And they continue to do so. Thanks to the adaptability of the myths, Greek mythology is alive and well. It will carry on entertaining and teaching us far into the future.

So this is Greek mythology: a collection of wonderful stories that generation after generation, and culture after culture, have found entertaining and meaningful enough to tell and retell, and to adapt to their circumstances. The title of this book is *What Is Greek Mythology?* not *What Was Greek Mythology?* That is because in some form or other, the Greek myths are still with us.

Timeline of Greek Mythology

800 BCE	Greek alphabet is developed
776 BCE	Ancient Olympic Games are founded
c. 700 BCE	Homer's *Iliad* is written down
c. 650 BCE	Homer's *Odyssey* is written down
	Hesiod's *Theogony* and *Works and Days* are written down
566 BCE	Panathenaea festival is founded in Athens
534 BCE	City Dionysia at Athens is expanded to seven days
468 BCE	Sophocles beats Aeschylus for the drama prize
465 BCE	The skene is added to Greek theaters
458 BCE	Aeschylus's *Oresteia* is performed for the first time
447–432 BCE	The Parthenon is built on the Athenian Acropolis
100 BCE	Romans are in control of the Mediterranean world
29–19 BCE	Virgil writes the *Aeneid*
c. 8 CE	Ovid writes the *Metamorphoses*
c. 1–100	*Bibliotheca* of Apollodorus is written

Timeline of the World

814 BCE	Phoenicians found the colony of Carthage in North Africa
781 BCE	Zhou dynasty begins in China
750 BCE	First Mayan cities are built in Mesoamerica
c. 620 BCE	Lydia (western Turkey) mints the first coins
600 BCE	Jainism spreads as a religion in India
586 BCE	Jerusalem is destroyed by Nebuchadnezzar, king of Babylonia
563 BCE	Siddhartha Gautama, the Buddha, is born
500 BCE	Pueblo people become a corn-growing culture
459 BCE	Ezra leads the Jewish people from Babylon to Jerusalem
451 BCE	The Twelve Tables, laws of the Roman Republic, are established
325 BCE	Greek Pytheas of Massalia (Marseilles, France) sails around the British Isles
200 BCE–500 CE	The Hopewell culture flourishes in eastern North America

Bibliography

Buxton, Richard. ***The Complete World of Greek Mythology***. London: Thames and Hudson, 2004.

Hesiod. ***Theogony, Works and Days***. Trans. M. L. West. Oxford: Oxford University Press, 1988.

Homer. ***The Iliad***. Trans. Martin Hammond. Harmondsworth: Penguin Books, 1987.

Homer. ***The Odyssey***. Trans. E. V. Rieu, D. C. H. Rieu. London: Penguin Books, 1991.

Morales, Helen. ***Classical Mythology: A Very Short Introduction***. New York: Oxford University Press, 2007.

Ovid. ***Metamorphoses***. Trans. A. D. Melville. Oxford: Oxford University Press, 1986.

Virgil. ***The Aeneid***. Trans. C. Day Lewis. Oxford: Oxford University Press, 1986.

Waterfield, Robin, and Kathryn Waterfield. ***The Greek Myths: Stories of the Greek Gods and Heroes Vividly Retold***. London: Quercus, 2011.